A Passion for Music

I Talk You Talk Press

Copyright © 2018 I Talk You Talk Press

ISBN: 978-4-907056-58-2

www.italkyoutalk.com

info@italkyoutalk.com

All rights reserved. No part of this publication may be resold, reproduced, stored in retrieval system, copied in any form or by any means, electronic, mechanical, photocopying, recording or otherwise transmitted without the prior written permission from the publisher. You must not circulate this publication in any format, online or otherwise.

This is a work of fiction. Names, characters, businesses, organizations, products, places, events and incidents are either the products of the author's imagination or are used in a fictitious manner. We have no affiliation with any existing companies mentioned in this story. Any resemblance to actual persons, living or dead, existing stories or actual events is purely coincidental.

Although the author and publisher have made every effort to ensure that the contents of this book were correct at press time, the author and publisher do not assume and hereby disclaim any liability to any party for any loss, damage, or disruption caused by errors or omissions, whether such errors or omissions result from negligence, accident, or any other cause.

Image copyright: © sumnersgraphicsinc #38565940 Standard License

CONTENTS

Chapter One	1
Chapter Two	4
Chapter Three	7
Chapter Four	10
Chapter Five	13
Chapter Six	17
Chapter Seven	21
Chapter Eight	24
Thank You	27
About the Author	29

CHAPTER ONE

Ben Grimes is fifteen years old. He lives in a small town near London with his mother and younger sister. He is quiet and shy. He doesn't have many friends. He doesn't like school or studying. He only likes music.

Ben plays the trumpet. He is a very good trumpet player. His mother cannot buy him a trumpet. They cost a lot of money. Ben's trumpet belongs to the local government. The trumpet is his best friend. He plays the trumpet every day. His sister doesn't like the trumpet. She thinks it is very noisy. Ben's mother works very hard in a supermarket every day. She is a very good mother to Ben and his sister. She doesn't have much money, but she gives Ben and his sister pocket money every week. She gives them £2 each. Ben's sister buys sweets with her £2. Ben saves his. When he is older, he wants to buy his own trumpet.

Ben gets up at 6:00am every morning. At 6:30, he goes to the park. In the park, he plays his trumpet. He cannot play his trumpet at home because his sister and his neighbours get angry.

They say, "It's too noisy!"

He plays his trumpet in the park until 8:00am. Then, he goes to school. He does not study hard at school. He dreams about his future. In the future, he will be a great trumpet player. He will be rich and famous. He will buy his mother a house. His mother will be very happy.

Ben's teachers are always angry. They say, "Stop dreaming! Study!" But Ben can't stop dreaming, or thinking about his trumpet.

At lunchtime, Ben doesn't play with the other children. He eats his lunch very quickly, and then goes to the music room to practice the trumpet.

After school, Ben goes home. His mother works in the supermarket until 10:00pm, so Ben has to cook dinner for his younger sister every day. After dinner he listens to classical music or jazz music. He shares his bedroom with his sister. She doesn't like Ben's music. She likes pop music. So, every night, Ben listens to music on an old portable CD player.

At school, Ben has a trumpet lesson once a week. A trumpet teacher comes to his school every Tuesday. His trumpet teacher, Ms Jones, is a professional trumpet player. She plays in a jazz band.

Ben's trumpet lessons are free. In Ben's town, there is a government music education programme. The government music education programme pays for children's music lessons. Also, Ben borrows a trumpet from the government music education programme. Ben doesn't want to borrow a trumpet. He wants his own trumpet. He wants to buy a trumpet. On Saturday afternoons, he goes into the town centre. He stands outside the music shop and looks at the trumpets in the window. He dreams about buying a trumpet, but the trumpets in the shop are too expensive for his family.

Today is Tuesday. He is happy because he has a trumpet lesson with Ms Jones. He goes to the music room.

"Good morning Ms Jones."

"Good morning Ben," says Ms Jones.

Ben looks at Ms Jones. She doesn't look very happy.

"Are you OK Ms Jones? You look sad," says Ben.

"Ben, I have some bad news," says Ms Jones.

"Bad news? What is it?" asks Ben. "What's happened?"

"Oh Ben, I'm very sorry," says Ms Jones. "Up to now, the government has paid for your trumpet lessons. The government lends you a trumpet. It's a very good system. But the government has no money. It can't pay for your music lessons anymore. The music education programme will finish."

"Finish? So, I can't have trumpet lessons anymore?" asks Ben.

"I'm sorry, Ben. You can't have free trumpet lessons anymore. If you want trumpet lessons, you will have to pay for the lessons. And, you will have to buy your own trumpet. I'm very sorry," says Ms Jones.

Ben is very shocked. He sits down on the chair next to Ms Jones.

"But, I can't buy a trumpet! I can't pay for lessons! They are too expensive! Please help me, Ms Jones, please help me!"

Ben starts to cry, and Ms Jones feels bad. She wants to help Ben, but he can't pay for lessons and she can't give him free lessons.

That night, Ben goes home and talks to his mother. He tells his mother the bad news.

"Mum, I want to play the trumpet. I want to have trumpet lessons," says Ben.

"I'm sorry, Ben. I can't pay for trumpet lessons. The lessons are too expensive, and trumpets are very expensive. I can't buy you a trumpet," says his mother.

"I know. I understand," says Ben. "But what am I going to do?"

"In the future, when you start working, you can save your money and buy a trumpet. Then, you can play the trumpet again," says his mother.

"But I want to be a trumpet player! I don't want another job! I can't do anything else!" says Ben. "One day, I'll be famous and rich, and we can be happy!"

"I'm sorry Ben. But life is hard. You will understand when you are older," says his mother. Ben goes to his bedroom and gets into bed. He cries all night.

The next day, a man from the government education programme comes to his house. The man takes the trumpet. The government will sell the trumpet to another student. Her name is Emma. Emma's family is rich. Emma's parents will buy the trumpet and pay for lessons.

Ben is very sad because the trumpet is his best friend. He holds the trumpet for the last time. He says, "goodbye my friend," and then he gives the trumpet to the man.

CHAPTER TWO

The next Saturday, Ben goes into the town centre. He goes to the music shop and looks at the instruments in the shop window. There is a beautiful silver trumpet in the window. He looks at the price. £1,000. He goes into the shop.

"Excuse me," he says to the man in the shop. "Can I look at that trumpet, please?"

"Yes, of course," says the man. He takes the trumpet from the window display and gives it to Ben.

Ben starts to play. He feels so happy playing the trumpet again. Ten minutes pass. Then twenty minutes. Then thirty minutes.

"Excuse me," says the man. "Are you going to buy that trumpet?"

"I want to, but I can't. I don't have any money," says Ben.

"If you are not going to buy the trumpet, you can't play it. Give it back to me," says the man.

Ben gives the trumpet to the man. He leaves the shop and goes home. In his bedroom, he listens to his CDs and dreams of the trumpet in the shop.

It is Monday.

Ms Jones comes to Ben's school to see Ben.

"How are you Ben?" she says.

"I'm OK, Ms Jones. But, I miss my trumpet very much. I really want to play the trumpet," he says.

"I know," says Ms Jones. "You are a very good trumpet player. If you have lessons, you will be an excellent trumpet player in the future.

Ben, I have some information for you," says Ms Jones.

"What kind of information?" asks Ben.

"There is a music competition in September. The first prize is £1000 and free lessons at the Professional School of Music every Saturday for a year. You are a very good trumpet player, Ben. I think you can win."

Ben looks at Ms Jones. *£1000! The trumpet in the shop is £1000. If I win, I can buy it! And, I can have free lessons at the Professional School of Music! But first, I have to win the competition. To win the competition, I have to practice,* he thinks. He looks at the calendar. It's July 2nd. There are two months until the competition.

"I think I can win. But I must practice. If I don't practice, I won't win. But I can't practice because I don't have a trumpet. Can I borrow your trumpet, Ms Jones?"

"I'm sorry Ben. I'm going to tour the USA in summer with my jazz band, so I can't lend you my trumpet. But I can lend you my trumpet in September for the competition."

"Thank you Ms Jones. But I need to practice. I need a trumpet in July and August."

"Well, if you find a trumpet, I think you can win the first prize," says Ms Jones.

"Thank you," says Ben. "I will find a trumpet. I must find a trumpet. I must win the competition!"

After school, Ben goes back to the music shop.

"Good afternoon," says the man. "Did you find some money? Do you want to buy the trumpet?"

"Not yet," says Ben. "How much is the cheapest trumpet?"

"The cheapest trumpet? Please wait a moment. I'll check for you," says the man. He looks at his computer.

"The cheapest trumpet is £500," says the man,

"£500…that's very expensive," says Ben.

"Yes, trumpets are expensive," says the man.

"How can I get money to buy a trumpet?" asks Ben.

"You could get a part-time job," says the man.

"A part-time job? Yes! That's a good idea!"

Ben runs out of the music shop and goes to every shop and restaurant in the town.

He asks the shop managers to give him a job, but all the shop and restaurant managers say "no". Ben is only fifteen, and there are many people in the town looking for jobs. There are no jobs for Ben. *What am I going to do?* thinks Ben. *I have to find a trumpet!*

CHAPTER THREE

It is Friday lunchtime. Ben is at school. It is a very sunny day and all the students are outside. They are playing football, or sitting on the grass, enjoying the hot weather. Ben is alone. He is always alone. Before, he played his trumpet at lunch time. Now, every day he walks around alone, thinking about the competition. He walks near the music rooms. He can hear the sound of a trumpet. It is Emma, playing the trumpet. Emma is not a very good trumpet player.

"My trumpet," says Ben sadly. "That's my trumpet! That trumpet was my best friend! I can play the trumpet better than Emma!"

The sound of the trumpet stops. Ben looks through the music room window. He sees Emma leave the room. She goes to the bathroom along the hall.

The trumpet is in the music room. Ben wants to touch the trumpet. He wants to hold it one more time. He wants to feel the trumpet on his lips. Ben looks around. The other students are playing and talking. No one is looking at him.

Ben jumps through the window and picks up the trumpet. His heart is beating fast. He feels very nervous. He holds the trumpet. The trumpet feels smooth and shiny. "My trumpet!" he says. "My trumpet!"

Then, he hears a sound. Emma is coming back! It's Emma! She will find him in the music room holding her trumpet! He panics and jumps out of the window.

Emma comes into the room and screams.

"My trumpet! Where is my trumpet?!"

Ben hides in the bushes. He is holding Emma's trumpet. His face is red, and he is sweating. His hands are shaking. He doesn't know what to do. He looks around. All the children are walking back into school. He hears the bell ring. Lunch time has finished. He puts the trumpet in the bushes next to the music room. He covers it with leaves. Then, he goes to his classroom.

In class, he doesn't listen to his teacher. He looks out of the window. He can see the music room.

Then, he sees a police car arrive at the school. The police car stops outside the music room. A policeman and a policewoman get out of the car. They walk into the music room. Ben starts to sweat and he feels his face turn bright red. He starts to panic.

Then, the head-teacher walks into the classroom.

"Good afternoon everyone," says Mr Singh.

"Good afternoon Mr Singh," say the students.

"I have some very serious news. Emma's trumpet has been stolen from the music room. Someone jumped through the window at lunchtime and took the trumpet. Emma is very, very upset," says Mr Singh. "We called the police. The police are looking for the criminal now."

Ben feels very nervous. He tries not to look around the classroom. He tries to stay calm, but his hands are shaking.

"Did you see anyone near the music room at lunch time?" asks Mr Singh.

The students shake their heads. "No, we didn't see anyone," say the students.

"Ben?" asks Mr Singh.

"What? Me? Yes? What?!" says Ben.

"You often go to the music room at lunchtime. Did you see anyone near the music room?" asks Mr Singh. Everyone looks at Ben.

"No…no, I didn't. I didn't see anyone," says Ben.

"Well, if anyone has any information, please tell me. We must find the trumpet and we must find the criminal," says Mr Singh.

Ben looks out of the window. He sees the teachers, Emma and Emma's mother. They are talking to the police officers. Emma is crying. They are standing next to the bush, and the trumpet. But they do not look in the bush, so they don't find the trumpet.

That night, Ben waits until his mother and sister are asleep. Then, he gets up very quietly and gets dressed. He goes out and walks to his school. The school gates are locked, so he climbs over the high wall. He jumps down and walks down the school path. It is very dark, but the moon is shining brightly. There is no sound, only the gentle wind in the trees.

He goes to the bush near the music room and finds the trumpet. He removes the leaves and dirt from the trumpet and cleans it with his shirt. He looks at the trumpet in the moonlight. It looks very shiny and beautiful. He holds the trumpet for a long time. He feels so happy holding the trumpet.

"My friend!" he says.

He starts to play the trumpet very quietly. He feels happy again. Then, he remembers Emma's face. She was very sad and she was crying. He feels bad again.

"No, Ben, this isn't right. This is very bad," he says to himself. "This trumpet is Emma's trumpet now. This is wrong," he says. "What can I do? I have to return the trumpet to Emma. But how can I return it?"

He sits on the grass in the moonlight and makes a plan.

He will come back to school on Saturday morning and practice the trumpet all day. Then, he will come back on Sunday and practice until late at night. He will go to school very early on Monday morning. He will put the trumpet outside the music room window. Emma will be very happy. No one will know about it. He can practice for two days, and Emma can get her trumpet back!

He goes home as the sky is starting to get light.

Ben goes back to school on Saturday and Sunday and practices the trumpet quietly. It feels good to play the trumpet again. He plays the music for the competition. By Sunday night, he is playing very well. He feels good. But on Monday, he must return the trumpet to Emma.

CHAPTER FOUR

It is Monday morning. Ben goes to school at 7:00am. It is very early, so there are no students and there are no teachers. He climbs over the wall and goes to the bush near the music room. He looks for the trumpet. It is not there!

"Where is it?!" Ben starts to panic. "Where is the trumpet?!"

Ben looks under the leaves. He looks around the other bushes and trees. He looks everywhere, but the trumpet is not there.

Ben sits down on the grass. He doesn't know what to do. Someone has stolen the trumpet. Very soon, all the students and teachers will arrive. What should he do? Should he tell his mother? Should he go to the police? He thinks for a few minutes.

He decides to tell the headmaster, Mr Singh. Mr Singh will be very angry, but he has to tell him. They have to find the trumpet.

Ben goes to the car park and waits for Mr Singh. At 8:00am, Mr Singh drives into the car park. He gets out of his car and walks into school. Ben follows him. He waits for Mr Singh to go into his office, and then he knocks on the door.

"Come in!" says Mr Singh.

Ben walks into Mr Singh's office.

He sits down on the chair opposite Mr Singh. He tells him the story. He tells him about the man from the government. He tells Mr Singh that he only wanted to hold the trumpet in the practice room, but Emma came back from the bathroom and he panicked. He tells him about his plan. He wanted to put the trumpet next to the music room window. But now, the trumpet is not there.

Mr Singh listens carefully to Ben. Then, he goes into the next room and comes back. He has the trumpet.

"The trumpet! Mr Singh, you have the trumpet!" Ben is very shocked. "Why do you have the trumpet?" he asks. "I don't understand."

"Last night, one of the teachers was walking her dog near the school. She heard the sound of a trumpet. She thought it was very strange. When she got home, she called me. An hour later, I came to the school, but I couldn't hear anything. So I searched the school grounds. I found the trumpet in the bushes," says Mr Singh. "Ben, you did a very bad thing."

"I know. I'm very sorry," says Ben. "I'm very sorry."

"This is Emma's trumpet, not yours. I understand your story. I know you love this trumpet. But, it is not your trumpet. You cannot take another person's trumpet," says Mr Singh.

"I know. I'm sorry. I really am. Are you going to tell my mother?" asks Ben.

"Yes, I am. I have to tell your mother," says Mr Singh. "And I want you to go to the police station and tell the police. Tell them you are sorry for wasting their time. And apologize to Emma. She is very upset."

Mr Singh calls Ben's mother. She is very angry.

"I work hard every day for you," she says. "I want you to be a good student and a good son. Why did you do this?"

"I don't know. I'm sorry. I just wanted to hold my trumpet," says Ben.

"The trumpet is not yours Ben! It's Emma's trumpet now. We don't have enough money to buy a trumpet," says his mother. "Forget the trumpet! Forget music! Study hard. Then, you can get a good job. Then, you can save your money and buy a trumpet."

Ben and his mother go to the police station. Ben says 'sorry' to the policeman and policewoman for wasting their time. The policeman tells him to be a good boy and to study hard.

The next day, Ben sees Emma.

"Emma, I'm very sorry. I did a very bad thing," he says.

Emma is angry.

"This is my trumpet now. Not yours," says Emma. "I never want to talk to you again! Go away!"

Emma tells the other students about Ben and the trumpet. The other students are angry. No one wants to talk to Ben at school. They call him bad names. They shout "Thief!" "Liar!" He spends every day alone, dreaming of his trumpet.

CHAPTER FIVE

School finishes and the long summer holidays start. Every day, Ben gets up early and goes for a walk in the park. He listens to music on his CD player all day. He thinks about his future. His mother said, "Forget the trumpet." But Ben does not want to forget the trumpet. He cannot forget it. He wants to be a famous trumpet player. He wants to study at the Professional School of Music. He wants to be rich because he wants to buy his mother a new house. He does not want to give up on his dream, but he has no money. *How can I get money? How can I buy a trumpet?* He thinks about this every day.

It is August 1st. Ben is eating his breakfast and reading the local newspaper. He sees an advertisement for a jewellery shop in the town centre.

Do you need money now? Sell us your jewellery! We will keep if for a month, and then you can buy it back!

He reads the advertisement one more time.
Do you need money now?
"Yes, I need money now," says Ben.
Sell us your jewellery! We will keep it for a month, and you can buy it back!
"Sell jewellery? Buy it back after a month?" says Ben. "I don't understand the system, but it sounds good....but, I don't have any jewellery."
Then he has an idea.

"My mother has some jewellery! It was her grandmother's and her mother's. So it's very old. She never wears it! I can sell my mother's jewellery, and then I can buy it back!"

He goes to his mother's bedroom. His mother's jewellery box is in a drawer. He opens it. There are many gold necklaces and bracelets in the box. They are beautiful. Ben takes the jewellery out of the jewellery box. He looks at the advertisement in the newspaper again.

We will keep if for a month, and you can buy it back!

Ben sits down on the chair and makes a plan.

I will sell the jewellery and then I will buy the £500 trumpet. Then, I will practice very hard, and win the competition in September. Then, I will go back to the jewellery shop and buy back the jewellery. Mum will not know about it! It's a great idea!

Ben takes his mother's jewellery to the shop. The man in the shop looks at it very carefully. Ben feels very nervous.

"Whose jewellery is this?" asks the man.

"It's my mother's jewellery," says Ben.

"Where is your mother?" asks the man.

"She is working today," says Ben. His face is red, and his hands are shaking. The man is asking many questions.

"How much money can I get?" asks Ben.

"Hmmm…some of this jewellery is very nice and very expensive. I can pay £500," says the man.

"And, can I buy it back?" asks Ben.

"Yes, you can," says the man. "Today is August 1st, so I will keep the jewellery until September 1st. If you don't come back before 4:00pm on September 1st, I will sell it."

September 1st is the day of the competition. Ben says, "OK, let's do it."

"OK, please tell your mother to come here. I need your mother's signature," says the man.

"What? You need my mother's signature? Why?" asks Ben.

"You are a young boy. This is a lot of money. So I need your mother's signature," says the man.

Ben thinks for a few seconds.

What can I do? I really need the money to buy a trumpet. But, my mother will be angry. I cannot ask for her signature. But I have to get the money! I need the money to buy a trumpet. What can I do? If I buy a trumpet, I can practice. If I practice, I can win the competition. If I win the competition, I can become a good trumpet player. If I become a good trumpet player I can get money. If I get money, I can buy my mother a house.

Ben has an idea. He knows it is a bad idea, but he needs the money.

"My mother is too busy to come here. Can I take this form home? My mother will sign it and I will bring it back here," says Ben.

"OK," says the man. He gives Ben the form. Ben runs home and sits at the table in the kitchen. He picks up a pen, and very carefully signs the form with his mother's name: Andrea Grimes.

Then, he goes back to the shop.

"Here is the form. My mother signed it," says Ben. He gives the man the jewellery and takes the £500.

He runs out of the shop. He is very excited. He has £500! He can buy a trumpet! He runs into the music shop in the next street.

"Can I buy the £500 trumpet, please?" he asks the man.

"Where did you find £500?" asks the man. He thinks it is very strange.

"My grandmother gave me the money," says Ben. He feels bad because it is a lie, but he really wants the trumpet.

He gives the man £500 and the man gives him the trumpet. When he holds the trumpet, he feels so happy.

My trumpet! I have a trumpet!

Ben feels very excited and runs to the park. He takes the trumpet out of its case and starts to play. He forgets about his mother's jewellery. He forgets about the signature. He sits in the park and plays for many hours.

At home, Ben hides the trumpet under his bed. He doesn't tell his mother or his sister about the trumpet. When his mother goes to work, he goes to the park and practices his trumpet for twelve hours every day.

One day, his mother is walking to work and she sees Ben playing the trumpet in the park.

"Ben! What are you doing? Whose trumpet is that?" asks his mother.

"Oh, mum!" Ben is very surprised. "Er…it's…it's… Ms Jones's trumpet," he says. "Ms Jones lent me a trumpet for the competition in September."

"Really? I will call Ms Jones to say 'thank you'," says his mother.

"No! No, er…Ms Jones is in the USA now," says Ben. He feels

very nervous. He doesn't like lying to his mother.

"Oh, I see. Well, she is very kind," says his mother.

Ben looks at his mother's face. She looks very tired. She works hard every day. Ben remembers the jewellery and he feels very bad.

If I don't win the competition, my mother will lose her grandmother's jewellery, he thinks. He starts to feel very worried. *I have to win the competition. I have to win!*

Ben practices every day from morning to night. His fingers hurt and his lips hurt. He feels very tired, but he can't rest. He needs to win the competition. He needs to win the money so he can buy his mother's jewellery back. He must win the competition at the Professional School of Music.

Summer passes, and the air is getting cooler. It is nearly September. Can Ben win the competition?

CHAPTER SIX

It is September 1st. Ben, his mother and his sister wake up very early. Ben is very nervous. The competition starts at 9:00am. They have to take the train into London. It will take forty-five minutes.

It is 7:30am. His mother is wearing a dress. She doesn't go to big events very often. She only has one dress and it is very old. She doesn't have enough money to buy a new dress.

"Come on, mum! We have to go now!" says Ben.

"Wait a minute! I can't find my necklace! That necklace was my grandmother's necklace. She gave it to me before she died," says his mother. She is in the bedroom looking for her necklace.

Oh no! thinks Ben. He starts to panic.

"Mum, you don't need a necklace! We have no time!" says Ben.

"But I need a necklace. Today is a very important day. I want to look nice. My dress is old. My shoes are old. I don't look nice. I need my necklace," she says.

"Mum, you look nice without the necklace! You look beautiful!" he says.

"Oh Ben! Do you think so? Thank you! You are a very good son!" says his mother.

Ben feels bad. If he doesn't win the competition, his mother will find out about the jewellery and she will think he is a very, very bad son. Ben feels a lot of pressure.

Ben, his mother and his sister arrive at the Professional School of Music. It is a very old and beautiful building. They walk into the lobby. There are many children there. Many children look very rich. The boys are wearing suits and the girls are wearing beautiful dresses. They are warming up. Some children are playing violins and some children are playing flutes. There are many kinds of instruments. Ben looks around the room. He sees Emma.

"Hello Emma!" he says.

Emma doesn't say hello. She doesn't smile. She doesn't look at him.

He sees Ms Jones.

"Ben! It's nice to see you!" says Ms Jones. "Did you find a trumpet?"

"Ms Jones! Thank you so much for lending Ben your trumpet!" says Ben's mother.

"Pardon? What do you mean?" asks Ms Jones. "I didn't lend…"

Ben starts to panic.

"Stop! Look at the time! Ms Jones, can you help me warm up?" he says quickly. "You can talk to my mother later."

"Of course," says Ms Jones. They go into a practice room.

"Ben, I don't understand. What is your mother talking about? My trumpet? I didn't lend you a trumpet."

Ms Jones looks at Ben's trumpet.

"Is that a new trumpet? Where did you get it? It looks expensive," says Ms Jones.

Ben tells Ms Jones about his mother's jewellery. Ms Jones is very shocked.

"Ben! That is terrible! That is very, very bad!" she says.

"I know. But, please don't tell my mother. In the future, I want to be a famous trumpet player. I will be rich. I will buy my mother a car, and a house. But, I have to win this competition!" says Ben.

"Let's talk about this later," says Ms Jones. "You did a very bad thing. But, it's too late now. Good luck in the competition. You have to win."

The competition starts. Ben watches the other children. Some of the children are very good. Some are not so good. He watches Emma play. She plays very badly.

Next, it is Ben's turn.

He hears the announcement "Next, Mr Ben Grimes!"

Ben walks on to the stage. He feels very nervous. The stage lights

A Passion for Music

are very bright. There are many people watching. He sees his mother and his sister. They are sitting at the front.

When Ben starts to play, he relaxes. He doesn't feel nervous anymore. He plays two pieces of music - a fast piece and a slow piece. He looks at his mother. She looks so proud. He closes his eyes and plays for his mother. He doesn't think about the money, or the jewellery. He only thinks about the music. He plays beautifully. He opens his eyes. Everyone is standing up and clapping. His mother is crying. Ms Jones is smiling. Ben smiles, takes a bow, and then walks off stage.

The competition finishes. Ben sits next to his mother, his sister and Ms Jones. His mother holds his hand. She is very proud of her son. Ben is very worried. He played very well, but many other children played very well too. The judges walk onto the stage. Everyone claps.

The head judge is a music teacher at the Professional School of Music. He stands at the microphone and starts to talk.

"The standard of playing was very high. Everyone played very well. Well done! The winner will get £1,000 and will study here, at the Professional School of Music every Saturday, for a year. Then, when the winner becomes eighteen, he or she can study here full-time for three years. This school has many famous teachers, and…"

Ben feels very nervous. He closes his eyes. He hates long speeches. He only wants to hear the winner's name!

At last, the head judge finishes his speech.

"And now, I will announce the winner. It was a very difficult decision because everyone played very well. But, the winner played very beautifully. The winner of this year's music competition is…Ben Grimes!"

Ben holds his head in his hands. He can't believe it. Everyone in the hall stands up and starts clapping. Ben's mother starts crying. Ms Jones starts crying too. His sister smiles at him. Ben walks up onto the stage and shakes hands with the judges. The judges give him an envelope. In the envelope there is £1,000 in cash. Ben smiles and holds the envelope very tightly. He cannot believe it. He won the competition.

Life is wonderful, he thinks.

Ben walks off stage and hugs his mother and Ms Jones.

Then, Ben remembers the jewellery.

"Mum, what time is it?" he asks.

"It's 3:30," says his mother.

"3:30? Oh no! The jewellery!" says Ben.

"What? Ben! Where are you going?" asks his mother.

"I have to do something! I'll see you later!" he says, and runs out of the Professional School of Music and across London to the train station.

CHAPTER SEVEN

Ben gets off the train and runs down the street and into the town centre. The jewellery shop closes at 5:00pm. He hopes the jewellery is still in the shop. He looks at the clock on the town hall. It's 4:50pm.

He runs into the shop.

"I have the money! Can I have the jewellery back please?" he asks.

"I'm sorry, you are too late. I told you to come back before 4:00pm. Someone just bought the jewellery," says the man.

"What? No! No! Who bought it?" asks Ben. He feels sick. What is he going to do?

The man looks out of the window.

"That woman getting into her car, over there," he says. "She bought it five minutes ago."

Ben runs out of the shop. There is a road between Ben and the car park. It is a very busy road and there are many cars. He can't cross the road.

"Stop!" shouts Ben. But the woman cannot hear him. She is reversing her car. Then, she drives away.

"No!" shouts Ben. He sees a taxi.

"Stop! Taxi!" says Ben.

The taxi stops and Ben gets in.

"Follow that car!" says Ben.

The taxi driver looks at Ben and laughs.

"What? Follow that car? This is not a Hollywood movie!" says the driver. "Where do you want to go? Tell me the address."

Ben pulls some money out of his coat.

"I'll pay you! Just follow that car!" he shouts.

The driver looks at the money. He is very surprised.

"OK, OK," he says and starts to drive after the woman's car.

Luckily, the woman drives slowly. It starts to rain. The taxi follows the woman for about ten minutes. Then, the woman stops outside a large house. Ben gives the taxi driver twenty pounds and runs out of the taxi.

He knocks on the car window. The woman is about the same age as Ben's mother.

The woman is very surprised. She looks at Ben. "What is it? What do you want?" she asks.

"Did you just buy some jewellery?" asks Ben.

"Yes, I did. Why?" asks the woman.

"Can I buy it from you?" asks Ben.

"Buy it from me? No, of course you can't!" says the woman.

"Please! Please! Please! I need the jewellery!" he says. Ben sits down on the road. It is raining, and the road is wet. He starts to cry.

The woman gets out of her car. She looks down at Ben.

"Are you OK?" asks the woman. "What's wrong?"

"That's my mother's jewellery! I sold it!" says Ben. He is crying very loudly.

"What?" says the woman. "Why did you sell your mother's jewellery?"

Ben tells the woman his story. When he finishes telling the story, the woman is very shocked.

"How much did you pay for the jewellery?" asks Ben.

"I paid £800," says the woman.

"If I give you £900, will you sell it to me? Please?" asks Ben. "Please say yes! Please say yes!"

The woman looks at Ben. He looks so young and very sad. She wants to help him, but she also wants the jewellery. She doesn't know what to do.

"Please! Please!" says Ben. "I want to help my mother. She works hard every day in a supermarket. I want to be a famous trumpet player. If I am a famous trumpet player, I can get lots of money. Then, I can buy my mother a big house. I want to help my mother! I want to be a good son! I want my mother to be proud of me!"

The woman looks at Ben. She thinks about the situation. She has a son. Her son is a little older than Ben. Her son never helps her. He never thinks about her. But Ben wants to help his mother. He did a bad thing, but he did it for his mother. He is a very good son really. She makes a decision.

"OK," says the woman. "I will sell it back to you."

She gives Ben the jewellery.

"Oh thank you! Thank you so much! Thank you!" says Ben.

He gives her £900.

"No, it's OK. Just £800 is enough," she says.

"No, no," says Ben. "Please take £900."

"No," says the woman. "If you give me £800, you have £200 left. Use the £200 to buy your mother a nice present."

"Thank you. Thank you so much," says Ben.

"You must become a good son. Study hard, practice hard and become a good trumpet player. Do it for your mother," she says.

Ben hugs the woman. Then, the woman takes Ben back into the town centre.

CHAPTER EIGHT

Ben goes shopping and then goes home. His mother is not home yet. He puts the jewellery back in his mother's jewellery box. He goes to the living room and lies on the sofa. He waits for his mother to come home.

The front door opens. It is his mother and his sister.

"Are you home Ben?" asks his mother.

"Yes, I am home," he says.

"Where are you?"

"I'm in the living room," says Ben.

Ben's mother walks into the living room.

"I'm so proud of you Ben. You played very well today. What are you going to buy with the £1000?" asks his mother.

"I'm going to buy the trumpet from Ms Jones," says Ben. He feels bad again. He doesn't like lying to his mother.

"How much is it?" asks his mother.

"It's £800," says Ben.

"And what about the £200?" asks his mother. "Are you going to buy some music? Some CDs?"

"No. I already spent it," says Ben.

"You already spent it? What did you buy?" asks his mother.

Ben goes to his room and comes back with a big box and some flowers.

"I bought some flowers for you," he says.

"Oh Ben, thank you!" says his mother. "But, flowers don't cost £200."

"I bought you a present too," he says. He gives her the box. She opens it.

"A dress and shoes! Oh, thank you Ben, thank you!" says his mother. "But, Ben, when will I wear these?" she asks.

"You can wear them when you come to my concerts. I promise to do my best and become a rich and famous musician. I promise to work hard, and I promise to be a good son," says Ben. "I will buy you a house. We will be happy together."

"Oh Ben. Sometimes you do bad things, and sometimes you are a bad boy, but really, you are a very good son!" says his mother.

Ben smiles and hugs his mother. He feels so relieved. Everything ended very well!

Then, the doorbell rings.

"I'll get it," says Ben.

He opens the door.

"Ms Jones! Hi..er...do you want to speak to me?" says Ben.

"Ben, I'd like to speak to you and your mother," says Ms Jones.

"What about?" asks Ben. He starts to feel worried.

"Ben, you have to tell your mother the truth about the trumpet and the jewellery," says Ms Jones.

"Who is it Ben?" asks his mother. She walks into the hall.

"Oh Ms Jones! Come in! Come in!" says Ben's mother. "Thank you so much for everything Ms Jones. Thanks to you, Ben could win the competition."

Ms Jones walks into the living room and they all sit down.

"Ms Grimes, Ben has something to tell you," says Ms Jones.

Ben's mother looks at Ben. "Ben? What is it? What do you have to tell me?" she asks.

Ben looks at the floor.

"Ben?" says Ms Jones quietly. "I know this is difficult, but you have to tell your mother."

"Tell me what? What is it?" asks Ben's mother.

Ben can't look at his mother. He shakes his head.

"Ben, please," says Ms Jones.

"OK," he says. He tells his mother about the jewellery and the trumpet. His mother listens.

When Ben finishes telling the story, he looks at his mother. She is crying.

Ben's mother looks at him. "Why do you do these things Ben?

First you stole Emma's trumpet. Then, you sold my jewellery. You even sold the necklace from my grandmother! Why? Why? I try very hard. I want you to be a good, kind person. I want you to think of others. Why did you do this?"

Ben starts to cry. "Because I want to make you proud of me! And I want to buy you a big house! I want to be a famous trumpet player, and I want lots of money! I don't want lots of money for myself. I want lots of money for you! I want to make you happy mum!"

"I believe you Ben. But you did a bad thing. So, I'm going to stop your pocket money for six months," says his mother. "Do you understand?"

"Yes, I understand," says Ben.

"Ms Grimes, Ben did a bad thing, but he did it because he loves you," says Ms Jones. "He isn't a bad boy. He has a very kind heart."

Ben sits next to his mother and hugs her.

"Oh Ben, promise me. Promise me you will never do this again," says his mother.

"I promise mum. I promise," says Ben. "I promise to be a good son! And I promise to buy you a big house when I become a famous trumpet player!"

THANK YOU

Thank you for reading A Passion for Music! We hope you enjoyed Ben's story. (Word count: 7,122)

There are quizzes about this book on our free study site I Talk You Talk Press EXTRA. http://italk-youtalk.com

If you would like to read more graded readers, please visit our website
http://www.italkyoutalk.com

Other Level 2 graded readers include
Adventure in Rome
Andre's Dream
Christmas Tales
Danger in Seattle
Don't Come Back
Finders Keepers…
Marcy's Bakery
Men's Konkatsu Tales
Salaryman Secrets!
Stories for Halloween
The Perfect Wedding
The House in the Forest

The School on Bolt Street
Train Travel
Trouble in Paris
Women's Konkatsu Tales

ABOUT THE AUTHOR

I Talk You Talk Press is a Japan-based publisher of language textbooks, graded readers and language learning/teaching resources.

Our team is made up of highly experienced language teachers and translators, who have all studied at least one additional language to an advanced level.

This experience enables us to design our materials from the perspective of both the teacher and the learner. We consult with both teachers and language learners when designing our textbooks and graded readers, and test our materials extensively in the classroom before publication.

We are a fast-growing press, and currently publish graded readers for learners of English. We publish new graded readers monthly.

www.ingramcontent.com/pod-product-compliance
Lightning Source LLC
Chambersburg PA
CBHW032005060426
42449CB00031B/811